Baseball
in Action

Sports in Action

Sarah Dann & John Crossingham

Crabtree Publishing Company

Created by Bobbie Kalman

**To my mom and dad, Pat and Bobbie Dann,
who always taught me to come out swinging**

Editor-in-Chief
Bobbie Kalman

Writing team
Sarah Dann
John Crossingham
Niki Walker

Managing editor
Lynda Hale

Editors
Kate Calder
Heather Levigne

Computer design
Lynda Hale
Niki Walker
Robert MacGregor (cover concept)

Consultant
Jim Gates, Library Director,
National Baseball Hall of Fame and
Museum, Cooperstown, New York

Special thanks to
Mr. John Childs, Mrs. Kajak, Ms. Ricciardelli, Shawn Knott, Tran Duy Binh,
Akins Fortune, Kristi Evenden, Lydia Zemaitis, Kelsey Westbrook, Michael
Zigomanis, Kyle Derry, Neil Bell, Ali Raza, Fatima Ahmed, Holly Morin,
Rachel Ward, Abby Hume, and Earl Haig Public School; Blake Malcolm;
Michael Caruso; Andy DeForest, President, St. Catharines Minor Baseball;
David T. Gagné

Photographs and reproductions
Jeff Carlick/SportsChrome: page 16; Marc Crabtree: page 31 (top); Bruce
Curtis: pages 3, 8 (top), 9 (top), 10, 15, 20, 22, 23, 27 (both), 31 (bottom); Larry
Rossignol: page 30; Robert Tringali/SportsChrome: pages 17, 26; other images
by Digital Stock and Eyewire, Inc.

Illustrations
Barbara Bedell: page 5; Trevor Morgan: pages 6-7, 10, 11, 17, 20;
Bonna Rouse: pages 12-13, 14, 15, 19, 21, 23, 25, 26, 29

Production coordinator
Hannelore Sotzek

Digital prepress
Embassy Graphics

Crabtree Publishing Company

PMB 16A	360 York Road	73 Lime Walk
350 Fifth Avenue,	RR 4	Headington,
Suite 3308	Niagara-on-the-Lake,	Oxford
New York, NY	Ontario, Canada	OX3 7AD
10118	L0S 1J0	United Kingdom

Cataloging in Publication Data
Dann, Sarah
  Baseball in action

(Sports in action)
Includes index.

ISBN 0-7787-0163-8 (library bound) ISBN 0-7787-0175-1 (pbk.)
This book introduces the techniques, equipment, rules, and safety
requirements of baseball.

1. Baseball —Juvenile literature. 2. Baseball —Training—Juvenile
literature. [1. Baseball.] I. Crossingham, John. II. Title. III. Series:
Kalman, Bobbie. Sports in action.

GV867.5.D26 2000   j796.357   LC 99-38037
                                                                                CIP

Contents

What is Baseball?

Baseball is a popular team sport played in North America and around the world. Two teams of nine players take turns **batting** and **fielding**. The batting team **bats**, or hits, the ball and runs around the **bases**. They score **runs**, or points, by touching all three bases and **home plate**. The fielding team catches the ball and tries to stop the other team from scoring. The team that scores the most runs wins.

Top and bottom

Baseball games are divided into nine **innings**. An inning is the period of time during which each team bats once. The **visiting** team bats in the **top** of an inning, and the **home** team bats in the **bottom** of an inning. Players on the team at bat continue hitting until three players are out. Then the fielding team takes its turn at bat.

(right) Children all across America have played Little League® baseball games since the 1940s.

History of a pastime

In the 1700s, British children played a game called **rounders**, or **feeder**, which was similar to baseball. Players used a stick to hit a rock and ran around three posts. British settlers brought this game to North America. In the 1800s, people began using cloth sacks filled with sand instead of posts, which caused injuries. Players called the sacks "bases" and soon the game became known as baseball. Today, baseball is known as America's national pastime.

Welcome to the Diamond

Baseball games are played on a field that has two areas—an **infield** and an **outfield**. The infield, or **diamond**, is an area marked with lines that connect two of the three bases to home plate. The outfield is the grassy playing area beyond the diamond.

In the field

When a team is fielding, each player has a different **position**, or job to do. Three players are in the outfield and four cover the infield. The pitcher plays on the pitcher's mound, and the catcher plays behind home plate.

Scoring a run

One player steps up to bat. If the batter hits the ball, he or she runs counterclockwise around the bases and toward home plate to score a run. The batter, who is now the runner, stays on the farthest base that he or she reaches until another batter hits the ball. The runner scores a run when he or she returns to home plate.

Ruler of the diamond

The **umpire** is in charge of enforcing the rules. He or she usually stands behind home plate and decides whether the pitches are **strikes** or **balls**. The umpire also determines whether a runner is **safe** or **out** at a base.

*The **outfield** is the area between the wall and the infield dirt.*

left fielder ———▶

*The **foul lines** are the side boundaries of the baseball field. If a batter hits the ball and it lands outside the foul lines, the ball is out-of-bounds and called a **foul ball**.*

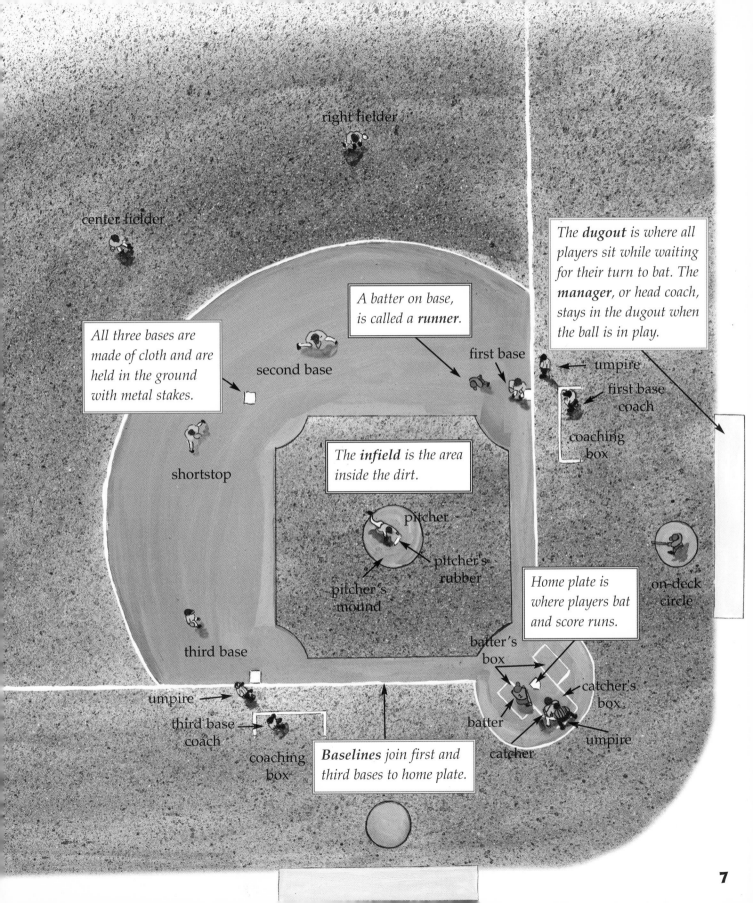

right fielder

center fielder

The **dugout** is where all players sit while waiting for their turn to bat. The **manager**, or head coach, stays in the dugout when the ball is in play.

A batter on base, is called a **runner**.

first base

All three bases are made of cloth and are held in the ground with metal stakes.

second base

umpire

first base coach

coaching box

shortstop

The **infield** is the area inside the dirt.

pitcher

pitcher's rubber

pitcher's mound

on-deck circle

Home plate is where players bat and score runs.

third base

batter's box

catcher's box

umpire

third base coach

coaching box

Baselines join first and third bases to home plate.

batter

catcher

umpire

7

Field Positions

The infielders are the first, second, and third base, and shortstop. They catch balls hit to the infield and **tag** or **force out** (see page 24) the runners. To tag a runner means to touch them with the ball to get them out. The outfielders— right, left, and center—catch balls that are hit to the outfield and throw them to the infield.

The pitcher...

The pitcher and catcher are known as the **battery**. It is the pitcher's job to **pitch**, or throw the ball across home plate. The pitcher has a strong arm for throwing the ball. He or she tries to throw difficult pitches in order to **strike out** the batter.

...and catcher

The catcher crouches behind the batter and catches balls that a batter does not hit. Catchers use hand signals to tell the pitcher which type of pitch to throw. A catcher also tries to tag runners when they head to home plate.

Covering the bases

The infielders try to stop the ball before it reaches the outfield. Once they get the ball, infielders throw to the base at which they have the best chance of getting a runner out. If a batter hits the ball to the infield, an infielder might throw the ball to first base to have the runner tagged or forced out. If a runner is heading for home plate, the infielders throw the ball to the catcher.

In the field

The left, right, and center fielders cover the outfield. Outfielders study a batter's **stance**, or body and bat positioning, and the type of pitch that the pitcher throws. They then try to guess the direction in which the ball is likely to go and prepare to catch it. Outfielders need strong legs for running after the ball and a powerful arm for throwing it quickly over long distances.

(top right) This first base player is waiting for the ball to tag this runner out.

(right) When a ball is hit to the outfield, the player nearest it should call "mine" so that the other outfielders won't run to catch it as well.

The Essentials

You do not need a lot of equipment to practice basic baseball skills—just a bat, ball, and glove. An actual game, however, requires more equipment such as three bases, a home plate, a batting helmet, and gloves for all the fielders.

*All players must wear a hard, plastic **batting helmet** while batting and running. The helmet helps protect your head if you get hit by the ball.*

*The **peak** of baseball caps and batting helmets shade a player's eyes from bright sunlight.*

peak

Catchers wear a mask, a chest protector, and shin guards in case they are hit with the ball.

Short-sleeved shirts allow players to move easily when batting and throwing.

Baseball pants are made of stretchy fabric to allow a player to run and slide easily.

stirrups

Sanitaries, or baseball socks, are white.

*Baseball shoes have short, plastic spikes called **cleats** on the soles. They provide a better grip on the field.*

Stirrups are colorful straps that are worn over a player's sanitaries.

The ball

Baseballs are small and hard. The cover is made of leather. The inside of the the ball is made of cork and rubber and tightly wrapped in wool yarn.

The bat

Major League players use wooden bats, but you can practice with an aluminum bat. Make sure the bat is light enough for you to swing easily. If the bat is too heavy, you will have trouble hitting.

Ball gloves

Leather baseball gloves protect your hands and make it easier to catch the ball. There are many different styles, but all gloves have long fingers and a woven pocket.

The first base player uses a glove with a deep pocket to provide a large target and scoop for catching the ball.

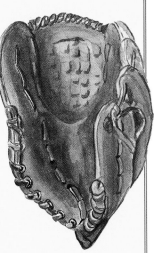

An infielder's glove has a small pocket so that the player can quickly grab the ball to throw it. Outfielder's gloves are similar, only larger.

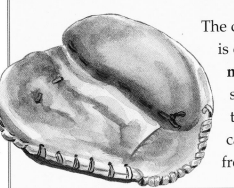

The catcher's glove is often called a **mitt**. A mitt has soft padding to prevent a catcher's hand from bruising.

Warming Up

Before practicing or playing, it is important to warm up and stretch your muscles. Warming up helps prevent injuries such as strains and pulls. It also gets your body ready to make hits, run bases, and throw the ball. The following stretches will help you warm up before you try the **drills**, or exercises, found in this book.

Trunk circles

Place your feet shoulder-width apart and put your hands on your hips. Keep your feet flat on the ground and swing your hips around in circles. Do three circles to the right and three to the left.

Leg crossovers

Stand with your legs crossed at the ankles. Slowly reach for your toes. Your knees should be slightly bent. Reach as far as you can. Hold for five seconds. Cross your other foot over your other leg. Do five stretches on each leg.

Ankle stretch

Sit on the ground and bend one leg so that you can grab your foot. Gently move it in circles away from you. When you've done ten circles away from you, stop and do ten toward you. Then do the same with the other foot.

Arm circles

Swing your arms in large circles. Keep making the circles smaller. Don't stop until your arms are out to the side and you are making tiny circles. Change direction. Start with small circles and finish with big ones.

"V" stretch

Sit with your legs in a "V." Stretch your arms as far as you can in front of you. Hold the stretch for a count of ten and then straighten up. Repeat five times.

Neck stretch

Tilt your head forward so that your chin points down toward your chest. Slowly roll your head to one shoulder and then the other. Only move your head as far as your shoulder and do not move it farther than feels comfortable. Never bend it back!

Leg lunges

Spread your feet apart as far as you can. Bend one knee and keep the other leg straight. Rest your hands on the bent knee and count slowly to five. Do five lunges to each side.

Batter up!

Batting requires a lot of practice. In order to hit the ball well, you need to develop a swing that is smooth and strong. Skilled batters can hit the ball so hard that they send it out of the ballpark! A few can even control the direction in which they send it.

If the ball is heading for your **strike zone**, as shown below, the pitch counts as a strike whether or not you swing. If the pitch is outside the strike zone, and you don't swing, it counts as a **ball**. If a pitcher throws four balls the batter gets to walk to first base.

Practice makes perfect

1. Wait in the batting stance for a pitch with your feet apart and knees slightly bent. Grip the bat with your hands one above the other and your fingers together. Your hands should be as high as your back shoulder. Get comfortable in this position. Do not rest the bat on your shoulder.

2. Bring the bat forward and shift your weight from your back foot to your front foot. Your back foot will turn, lifting your heel off the ground. Twist your hips as you swing so your lower body faces the pitcher. Keep your eye on the ball and swing the bat over the plate.

3. After hitting the ball, be sure to **follow through**, or continue swinging the bat around you to your opposite shoulder. Now drop the bat—never throw it—and run as fast as you can to first base.

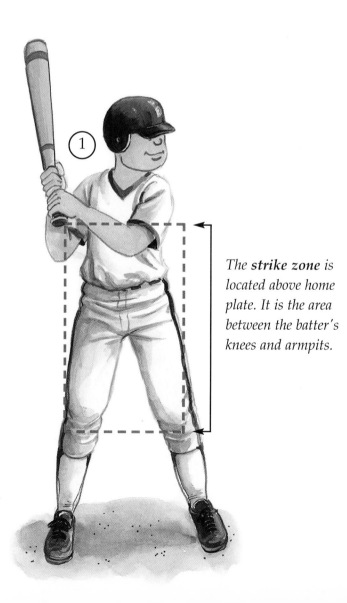

*The **strike zone** is located above home plate. It is the area between the batter's knees and armpits.*

Ball or strike?

Each time you swing and miss you get a strike. All batters dread getting three strikes and losing their turn at bat. Foul balls also count as strikes, but most do not count as a third strike (see page 18.) You don't have to swing at every pitch, but when the pitcher throws the ball you have only a split second to decide whether or not you can hit it.

(right) This pitch is too low and not in the strike zone. The batter is not swinging, so the pitch is a ball.

Take a Swing

Learning how and when to swing the bat is the first step in becoming an excellent batter. Everyone dreams of hitting the ball out of the park and scoring a **home run**, but there are other ways to hit the ball. Hitting the ball hard and straight into the air or smoothly over the ground are also useful for scoring runs. Controlling the direction in which the ball goes is also important because you can aim for a spot that isn't covered by a fielder.

Hit the middle

When batting, try to hit the middle of the ball as this boy has done. His hit will travel quickly over the infielders and then hit the ground before an outfielder can catch it. This type of hit is called a **line drive**. Avoid hitting the top or bottom of the ball. When hit on the top, a ball will be a **grounder**. Grounders bounce along the ground and are easier for fielders to pick up. When hit on the bottom, the ball will be a **fly ball**. Fly balls soar high into the air, giving fielders plenty of time to catch them.

Soft toss

Try swinging the bat through your strike zone. When you feel comfortable with your swing, try hitting a moving ball. Ask a partner to toss a ball to you. Stand in the batting stance, watch the ball closely, and give the bat a full swing. Remember to follow through. Did you hit it?

When you can hit a pitch almost every time, try hitting the ball in different directions. Set up three targets—one to the left, one to the right, and one straight ahead. Try to send the ball toward each one. Which target is the easiest to hit?

(top) Going to the park with a parent and some friends is a fun way to practice your batting, fielding, and throwing skills. All you need is bat, ball, and a couple of gloves.

17

Bunting

Batters usually hit the ball as hard as they can, but sometimes they trick the fielders by tapping it. This tap is called a **bunt**. Bunting forces the infielders to run forward to grab the ball and gives the batter more time to make it to first base. When bunting, try to tap the ball toward the baselines. If the ball rolls too far, an infielder will pick it up quickly and get you out. If you don't bunt it hard enough, the catcher will grab it and throw it to first base.

Even when you are planning to bunt, stand in the batting stance to fool the fielders. As soon as the pitcher pulls the ball behind his or her head, move your feet so they face forward and slide your top hand about halfway up the bat. Bring the bat up as high as your chest. Hold the bat away from your body but keep your elbows close to your sides.

A batter must be careful when bunting with two strikes— if he or she bunts a foul ball then it is a third strike.

A softer touch

Bunting requires a much softer touch than batting. When the ball hits the bat, pull back on the bat with your top hand. This movement will keep the ball from bouncing hard off the bat. Remember, you don't want to hit the ball far. To develop your soft touch, make a line about five giant steps from where you will be standing. Ask a friend to toss you the ball and try to bunt it so that it doesn't go past the line.

Remember to keep your hand behind the bat to avoid injuring your fingers.

*A player may make a **sacrifice bunt** when his or her team has fewer than two outs and a runner on base. Even though the bunter is often tagged out at first base, the other runner moves to second base. The runner is now in a good position to score on the next hit.*

Running the Bases

After you hit the ball, the next step is to make it safely to first base. When you make it there, you can decide whether or not to run to the other bases or even home plate. To get from base to base, you need to run fast and make quick decisions. When you are on base and the batter hits the ball you have to be ready to run to the next base. Your **base coach** will tell you when to run and when to stay.

The runner below has crossed home plate before a fielder could throw the ball to the catcher. The umpire is waving out both arms as a signal that the runner is safe.

Don't stop!

A runner who isn't touching the base can be tagged out. To be tagged out, you must be touched by an opponent who has the ball. The one exception to this rule is when you are running to first base. In order to run as fast as possible, you can run straight over the base without stopping and then slow down after you have touched first base. The first base player cannot tag you before you return to the base.

You're out! This fielder got the ball in time to tag the runner's foot.

Running the line

When you are running around the bases you must stay along the baseline. You are not allowed to run more than three feet (1 m) off the line.

If the runner and the ball arrive at a base at the same time, the umpire decides whether the runner is safe or out.

Stealing and Sliding

When you are standing on a base, it may seem like a long way to run to the next. Outrunning a swiftly-thrown ball can be difficult, so runners have a couple of tricks to help them get to the next base faster. Many runners give themselves a head start by taking a **lead off**. They stand a few steps off the base. Lead offs are not allowed in Little League.

Look before you leap

You must be careful when you have a lead off because you can be tagged out. The pitcher always keeps an eye on runners, and if you get too far off your base, he or she will turn and quickly throw the ball to the base player. You must run back and touch the base or you'll be tagged out.

Sliding

Sliding makes it more difficult for the player on base to tag you out because you extend your foot before the rest of your body. Your foot is a smaller target, so it is harder to tag. To slide, run and then stick out one leg straight in front of you. At the same time, pull your back leg off the ground and tuck it under your front leg. To do this, lean back, keep your head and shoulders upright, and face forward. Your backside should hit the ground first and not the knee tucked under your leg.

Stop, thief!

Instead of waiting for a batter to get a hit, a runner may decide to steal a base. Before you steal a base, and if allowed, take a good lead off. You must pay close attention to the pitcher. When you are sure the ball has left the pitcher's hand, run as fast as you can to the next base. In a few seconds, the pitch will reach the catcher's mitt, and he or she will try to throw you out. Don't look back until you reach the base—looking back will only slow you down.

This runner got caught stealing home. She's trying to make it back to third without getting tagged by the catcher.

Fielding

The team who is fielding focuses on getting three opponents out as quickly as possible. Fielders must have sharp reflexes to catch whatever type of hit or throw comes their way. If you miss the ball, it could cost your team runs!

You're out!

There are three ways for a fielder to get an opponent out. The first is to catch a hit before the ball touches the ground. The second is to tag a runner out. To tag the runner, you have to touch the runner with the ball or your glove with the ball inside it. The final way to get a runner out is called a **force play**.

Force play

Two runners cannot be on the same base. If there is a runner on first base, and the batter gets a hit, the runner must advance to second base to make room for the runner coming to first base. When a runner is being forced to run from one base to another and a player on base with the ball touches the base before the runner gets there, the runner has been forced out.

This outfielder is catching a fly ball before it goes out of the ball park.

Catching flies

Catching a fly ball requires concentration. Run with your head up and watch the ball. Continue running until you are under the ball and reach up to catch it. The fingers of your glove should point up. Put your other hand behind your glove to balance it and keep it steady. After you catch the ball, look to see where you should throw it. Make sure you wait until you have caught the ball before you look around or you may get hit by the ball.

Digging up a grounder

Grounders look easy to catch, but they can make odd bounces and hops over uneven ground. Be ready to move left or right as the ball approaches. Always stand in front of the ball in order to catch it.

To get used to grabbing grounders, ask a friend to toss or roll the ball to either side of you. Run to stop the ball, and then throw it back to your partner. When you master grounders, move on to fly balls. Remember to move to meet the ball.

Throwing

Throwing is a major part of fielding. When the ball is hit your way and a runner is approaching the base, it is up to you to catch the ball and throw it quickly and accurately to the correct base. If your teammate cannot catch the ball, he or she cannot get the runner out.

(left) This player is concentrating on his target. Learn how to throw the ball without becoming distracted.

Face your target. Bring the ball behind your head and twist at your waist. Your non-throwing shoulder should point at your target. All your weight should be your back foot.

As you step forward, bring your throwing arm forward in a big circular motion. Your body will twist as you throw, bringing your back shoulder forward. Keep your head up and look at your target. Release the ball when it is in front of you. Let your arm follow through and complete its circle.

Don't crack under pressure!

It is easy to get nervous when the score is close. Some players get anxious and they miss the ball, drop it, or throw it in the wrong direction. These mistakes can cause their team to miss getting a player out.

To practice throwing under pressure, toss a ball back and forth with a friend and pretend it is on fire. The idea is to get rid of the ball almost as soon as it touches your glove. Try to aim well so that neither of you misses the ball or has to move far to catch it.

This second-base player waited for a throw that never came! The runner slid safely to the base.

The overthrow

Sometimes a player throws the ball in a hurry and does not aim well. When this happens, the ball may be **overthrown**, or go over the player's head. The player at third base, pictured right, is stretching to catch an overthrow. His teammate threw the ball too high and too hard. In the meantime, the runner slides safely to the base.

Pitching

Pitching is the most difficult baseball skill to master. Pitchers must throw balls that are difficult to hit but still reach the strike zone. They try to throw a variety of pitches to fool the batter. Fast balls, **curve balls**, **screw balls**, **knuckle balls**, and **change-ups** are different types of pitches that are used to surprise the batter.

The pitching motion

It is important to **windup**, or prepare for the pitch, properly. In your spare time, you can practice these motions without a ball. Stand in front of a mirror and practice your windup slowly. Watch experienced pitchers and study how they move.

Pitching the ball accurately takes practice. If a pitcher can't throw strikes, the team can't win!

Pitching form

1. Stand with both feet facing the batter. Take a step straight back with your left foot. As you step back, lift your hands just above your forehead.

2. Turn your front foot sideways and to the right. This motion is called the **pivot step**. Bring your left foot forward and lift the knee across the front of your body. You should now be balanced on one foot. Your hands are above the bent knee.

The fastball grip

Young pitchers should begin by throwing only fastballs—other pitches can injure your arm if you do not do them properly. These illustrations show the way to grip a ball when you are throwing a fastball.

3. Pull your throwing arm straight back and step toward the plate with your left leg. As you step, make a complete circle with your throwing arm. Release the ball as your foot hits the ground. Remember to follow through with your arm.

Different Ball Games

Other games have equipment and rules that are similar to baseball. **Cricket** is a popular game around the world and played with two teams of eleven players. A cricket bat is flatter and wider than a baseball bat. Instead of bases, cricket players run from one **wicket** to another to score runs. Two batters stand in the **bowling crease**. A **bowler** throws the ball overhand or underhand to one batter. Players in the field catch the ball with their bare hands and throw it at the wicket. Knocking the **bail**, or top rail, off the wicket gets the batter out.

Closer relatives

Other games also use a bat and ball. Many of these games, which are almost identical to baseball, are popular in North America as well as the rest of the world.

Different pitches

The difference between most ball games is the style of pitching. In **softball**, pitchers use a larger ball that they throw underhand. The pitcher stands closer to the batter than in baseball, and the bases are closer together. **Slow pitch** is a game with rules similar to those of softball, but pitchers **lob** the ball, or toss it high and slow, to the batter.

*(above) In **teeball**, there is no pitching at all! Many young players play teeball before baseball to learn the basics of batting.*

Softball is popular both with young players and adults. Many countries have men's and women's national teams.

21738

Baseball Words

ball A pitch at which a batter does not swing and does not pass through the strike zone

base A bag or plate that marks one of the four corners of a baseball diamond

base coach A coach who stands near first or third base and instructs the runners when to run

bottom Describing the second half of an inning in which the home team is up to bat

change-up A pitch that appears to be a fast ball but travels much slower

curve ball A pitch that curves in the opposite direction from the pitcher's throwing arm

fielding Retrieving the ball in an attempt to get batters out

force out A play in which a runner must advance to the next base and a fielder with the ball touches the base first

home run An hit that enables the batter to run and touch all four bases without being tagged out

knuckle ball A slow pitch with lots of movement created by gripping the ball with the fingertips

lead off Standing a few steps off the base to get a head start at running to the next base

out Describing a player who is put out of play by the opposing team

overthrow A throw that goes farther than its target

safe Describing a player who gets on base successfully

screw ball A pitch that curves in a direction opposite to a curve ball

strike An attempted swing at the ball that fails; A ball that is pitched into the strike zone

strike out Three strikes thrown by the pitcher, putting the batter out

tag An action in which a fielder who has the ball touches a runner who is off base to get him or her out

top Describing the first half of an inning in which the visiting team is up to bat

Index

32   1 2 3 4 5 6 7 8 9 0 Printed in the U.S.A. 8 7 6 5 4 3 2 1 0 9